Be The Creator of Your Success NOT A Victim of Your Circumstances

12 Steps To Creating the Life You Were Destined to Live

Keisha A. Rivers Shorty

Copyright © 2014 Keisha A. Rivers Shorty, The KARS Group LTD

www.karsgroup.com   www.releasedandready.com

All rights reserved.

ISBN: 0615707017
ISBN-13: 978-0615707013

DEDICATION

This book is dedicated to those who are seeking the courage to change their lives for the better. To those who have wondered if there was more and who are taking their first step by picking up this book.

It is presented as a labor of love to those who need to hear the words in order to feel the ripple effect of change.

You are more than enough.
Live. Laugh. Love.

~Keisha

KEISHA A. RIVERS SHORTY

SPECIAL THANKS

This is a word of special thanks that goes out to the people in my life who have been there throughout my journey.

It is because of knowing you and because of your support and belief in me that I have become the woman that I am today—and have arrived in this moment.

Thank you.

~Keisha

HOW TO USE THIS BOOK

As Book 1 in the *Release Yourself*™ *Series* of The KARS Paperback Coaching Library that includes The Released & Ready™ Personal & Professional Development Modules, this book is meant not only to be a "good read"—entertaining, enlightening and educational—but also to serve as a step-by-step guide in helping you shift your thinking, develop action plans and begin your journey to change your life.

Because they are meant to accompany you on your journey, each book in the Series is designed as a guide that you will use to create and implement the new systems that you'll need along the way. Each chapter represents a theme or concept that you will use in outlining the steps that will assist you in taking your vision from conception to reality.

As you read through the chapters you should reflect upon the issues addressed and identify areas within your own life where you need to make some changes. <u>Keep a journal or notebook handy to write down your thoughts. This is an active process so don't just read the book—but actively think about what's being said and write down your own thoughts and experiences along the way.</u> At the conclusion of the book, there is a strategy development chapter where you will be able to create your own action plan and make some decisions about moving forward.

There is no test at the end of the book; and there is no way that anyone will know whether you completed the exercises or not—after all, I'm not going to come and "check your homework" so to speak. But YOU will know whether you wholeheartedly participated in the process by the outcomes that you begin to see and create in your life.

Don't let fear hold you back. You've taken the first step by buying, downloading or picking up this book. That means you are ready for a change—and that's crucial to laying the foundation for a good beginning.

Now you just need to go through the journey. Don't worry about what you have, don't have or need. You already have what's most important—
YOURSELF.

You are more than enough.

Take a deep breath. Exhale slowly.
Now begin.

CONTENTS

Welcome

1   Be the Creator Of Your Success   Pg 1

2   The Boogeyman Doesn't Live Here Anymore: Pg 26
       Evicting the Element of Fear

3   The Message in the Mirror: Pg 32
       Self-Talk & The Power of Language

4   Deconstruct to Reconstruct: Pg 37
       Dissecting The Vision: Laying The Path

5   Cooperation & Collaboration: Pg 46
       Building The Team You Need

6   Reflection, Redirection & Release: Pg 51
       Making Decisions; Taking Action

7   12 Steps: Pg 57
       Creating The Life You Were Destined To Live

> *Note 2 Self: "Don't let the fear of the greatness that is within you stop you from being the greatest you." ~KARS*

Welcome to the beginning of the rest of your life!

Sometimes the potential that we see or feel within ourselves--and especially the potential that others see within us--is so far beyond what we envision for ourselves that we run from it.

It doesn't matter what kind of car you drive right now, what kind of house you live in, where you work--or don't work, what you look like, what you sound like, where you went to school, where you're from, what you don't have or even what you do.

The bottom line is that you have to tell yourself--and believe--that you ALREADY ARE the wonderful, exceptional, talented, gifted person that you are afraid to be. You just have to set yourself free-- RELEASE YOURSELF--and get out of your own way.

Just because things have happened TO you, does not mean that those things DEFINE you.

It IS possible to move beyond, above and past the things of your past and those circumstances that comprise your present.

All you have to do is make a decision that you will be successful, profitable, joyful and start living the life that is meant for you.

It is a process.

It is a journey.

It is up to you.

I can assist you.

You've picked up this book (or downloaded it, as the case may be) because you are sick and tired.

Sick and tired of feeling overwhelmed, under-appreciated and unfulfilled.

Sick and tired of always putting yourself last because of everyday occurrences when "LIFE HAPPENS".

Sick and tired of feeling that everything in the universe seems to work *against* you instead of *for* you.

Sick and tired of feeling that there is something more out there for you that you are just not tapping into.

Sick and tired of having that feeling that you're not doing what you're meant to be doing with your life and that you're not at all where you think you should be.

But being sick and tired is not enough.

It is—however--just the beginning.

This book is the next step.

This book is about taking a journey. A journey to discover who you *really* are so you can get what you really want and go where you really want to be in life.

It's about changing not only your attitudes, but your *actions* as well so that you can create a new expectation, a new model and a new reality for your life and all aspects in it.

It's about waking up to a new day where you take on life's happenings as "opportunities" and "challenges" and you can…

"Be The Creator of Your Success, NOT A Victim of Your Circumstances"

Ready? Let's go! *~Keisha*

1. BE THE CREATOR OF YOUR SUCCESS

NOT A Victim of Your Circumstances

> *Note 2 Self: "You are more than the sum of your circumstances." ~KARS*

I know what you're thinking--"You don't know my circumstances."

Let me say this. It doesn't matter whether I know your circumstances or not. What I'm telling you is that whatever your circumstances—whatever it is that you are facing—if you are committed to being the creator of your success and making a *decision* to no longer being a victim of your circumstances, then you can and will create the life that you are destined to live.

The message and the strategies in this book are just the tools. The process starts with you.

If you don't *believe* it, if you don't whole-heartedly *want* it and *commit* to it, then nothing I say or do is going to make any difference whatsoever.

Let me tell you a secret—all of the coaches, strategists, self-help books, courses, seminars, trainings, retreats, programs or any other products that are designed to "change your life" don't mean a hill of beans if YOU don't make a *decision* to change and then *honor* those decisions with action.

I'm not here to tell you that it's going to be easy. I'm not going to tell you that you're not going to have days when you're going to want to give up. What I **will** tell you is that it will be worth it and that you will thank me--and yourself once you come through it.

Now, let me tell you what this is and what it isn't.

This is **not** a purely motivational book filled with cute little stories and tear-jerkers that will touch you emotionally and get you pumped up but not much else.

What this *is*—is a strategy guide that provides you with information, tips and insights to help you to identify those things that keep you from addressing the circumstances in your life, overcoming them and moving past them.

Does it include some of what would be considered motivational and inspirational stories, examples and sayings? Yes. Is that all there is to this? Absolutely not.

The bottom line is that in making the *decision* to become the creator of your success instead of remaining a victim of your circumstances, you are serving notice that you are no longer willing to just remain sick and tired for the sake of being sick and tired.

You are no longer going to remain frustrated, unfulfilled, unhappy, wondering "why you" or seeking validation, confirmation and affirmation from other people, situations or circumstances that are not--and have not--been created to fuel your passion, align with your purpose or build your legacy.

You are making a decision to take action.

You are recognizing that this is a journey.

You are making a commitment to yourself that you are going to do the hard work that is necessary to *create* the success that you want to have in your life.

Because actually, if you really think about it, being a victim is easy.

I know, I know. I'm going to get a lot of backlash for that one. But it's true.

I know what you're screaming in your head—"Do you think I actually *want* to be this way?" "Do I *want* to go through the same things over and over again?" "What part of *my life* is *easy*?"—and so on and so forth. Whatever your protests, I've heard it all before. I've said the same things.

But the truth of the matter is that if you've remained a victim of your circumstances for any length of time, then you've taken the easy way out.

Being a victim and making a choice to roll over and not *do* anything to change your life is easy because it doesn't require any action--all you do is keep things exactly the same. Keep doing the same things, going to the same places, being around the same people, thinking the same way—and your life will remain—exactly—the--same.

Making a *decision* on the other hand—requires effort.

What do I mean by that?

When you *truly* make a decision, you have to *honor* that decision with *action*. It requires commitment. It requires you to do what's difficult even when you don't feel like it—day in and day out. It requires you to be honest with yourself when you'd rather hide behind smoke and mirrors and a myriad of excuses. Making decisions and taking action is the hard part. And for those who are destined to be the creators of their success, they do what's hard.

So before you take on this journey, you have to ask yourself a fundamental question: *"How badly do I want it?"*

Because based on the answer to that question, then you'll know how badly you'll be willing to keep going and push yourself when you don't necessarily feel like it. You'll know how dedicated you'll be to following through on the information, strategies and tips that I've presented in this book. You'll know whether you're even dedicated enough to finish this book.

I'm not trying to scare you. I'm not trying to discourage you. I'm being *real* with you.

As a personal and professional development strategist, I work with clients from all types of backgrounds who have various goals and they all have different things that they want to accomplish. But the truth is that no one can **make** anyone do anything.

The level of success or failure that anyone achieves is completely up to them.

I know that first-hand. I wrote this book because I was where you are.

I was sick and tired.

Not only that, but I was lying in a hospital bed in the most excruciating pain in my life—with tubes down my throat, hooked up to machines, battling a severe infection and facing the second of what would become three major surgeries in three and a half weeks, and a fourteen-day hospital stay.

I was mourning the loss of a business that I had built from the ground up because I would no longer be able to service my clients for who knows how long.

I was terrified because I was facing mounting medical expenses and a dwindling bank account with no income potential and wondering what it was going to do to my financial situation.

I was trying to be strong while dealing with agonizing physical pain from the infection and complications as my organs systematically began shutting down and my body turned on itself and betrayed me.

I was wondering what the future held for me as I contemplated what my life would look like—not only if I survived this ordeal—but whether I would be able to survive at all.

Now this wasn't my first major ordeal, mind you. This was just the one that prompted me to write this book.

There were others—being on a roof and stranded for five days during Hurricane Katrina, business failures, the daily ups and downs of living—and those myriad of circumstances that cause you to want to crawl into a corner, pull the covers up over your head and decide that today is **not** the day and that you can't be "strong" anymore.

I wrote this book because as I lay there on my back, with tears streaming down my face soaking my pillow, I understood that the words that were flooding through my brain and the title that came to me were not meant just for me, but were meant to be shared with others—to encourage them, to assist them and to show them the way.

I've been through my share (okay, *more* than my share) of setbacks and issues and circumstances where things did not go my way. But in each case, I had a decision to make. I could either let those circumstances define me, or I could *use* those circumstances to motivate me and compel me to be better than I was before.

So this isn't just about motivation. This isn't just me telling you things that are good "in theory".

This is about me sharing with you things that I've discovered in my journey and things that have worked for me and others that I've helped.

This is about you not feeling like you're the only one and that no one understands you or what you're going through.

This is about you having a guide through your journey out of your circumstances.

Everyone needs to feel as if they are relevant. That they matter. That there is someone out there who not only "gets them" but is there for them.

I can assist you. I can guide you.

But I cannot do it FOR you.

YOU have to make the decision that what you've experienced thus far in your life is not what you want.

YOU have to honor that decision with actions and a strategic plan to create the changes you want and desire.

The truth of the matter is that if you've made it to this point in the book, you've already begun. (Congratulations!)

Because believe it or not, even though I've been telling you a number of reasons why this process is going to be difficult, you're STILL reading.

What that tells me (and should tell YOU) is that even though you can see just how hard the road is ahead of you, you're still ready and willing to move forward—which is a good sign.

Now the real work begins!

The Journey Begins…

> *Note 2 Self: "When you can stare your adversity in the face; look it dead in the eyes and still press forward-- then you know that you are ready to begin the difficult work that is inherent and necessary to make real, long-lasting change."*
> *~KARS*

The Process of Change

One of the most common phrases that I hear from my clients is that they will begin the process of change "when" or "once"—as in "when this happens" or "once that happens".

You know what I mean.

You feel that you can't possibly make anything different happen in your life the way things currently are—so you have to wait until things are different in order to make something different happen, right? As in:

"I'll go back to school *when* my kids grow up."
"I'll take that class *once* my family is more supportive."
"I'll write that book *when* my financial situation improves."
"I'll apply for a new job *once* my husband/wife gets a promotion."
"I'll start taking better care of myself *when* I have more time."

The list goes on and on and on of what we *will* do and *should* do if and when and once things change in our lives.

But really, the truth of the matter is that your circumstances don't have to change in order for you to begin to create your success.

Let me say that again.

Your present circumstances do not have to change in order for you to begin to create your success.

Change is a process—not an event.

That means that it occurs little by little over time. You see the results of change at the end, but really all change is, is just the sum total of a series of small changes that take place a little at a time.

Take a moment to think about that.

The key to becoming a creator of your success—and not remaining a victim of your circumstances—is to shift your thinking and your mindset from **event-thinking** to **process-thinking**.

This requires a fundamental shift in the foundation of your very core so that you are not SOLELY focused on the "big picture" outcomes that everyone sees, but rather on making the sustained, smaller process changes that CREATE the ending outcomes that you desire.

In other words, take the "baby steps" and celebrate the "small victories" along the way as you build your new life.

This is the process of change.

It begins with a DECISION and continues with consistent ACTION.

(Yes, I know I've been repeating that phrase over and over again. So that should tell you that it's important. ☺)

Now I know you want to know how in the world you're supposed to start making decisions and honoring those decisions with consistent action so that you can change your life?

Simple--in order to experience long-lasting change, it is necessary for you to understand and undertake a five-step process:

1) Reflect on your patterns;
2) Redirect your path;
3) Refine your thinking;
4) Rejuvenate your spirit and
5) Release yourself to act.

You must understand that this is a ***process***—which means that it is something that needs to be implemented and followed-through consistently over time in order for you to see the results that you want.
It is not something that you can just start—and then stop—and then start again—and then stop—over and over again, and expect to see long-lasting, sustainable change.

We're not looking for the short-term blips on the radar here.

Our goal is to create something long-lasting and sustainable that endures over time because when something has truly been "changed" and is "different" that means that it's in its new state consistently, over time.

To get to that point, you have to be systematic and strategic about actively changing your behavior and therefore your circumstances.

So let me explain my five step process of change:

Step 1: Reflect on your patterns: In order to truly make any strides in changing your behavior, your circumstances or to create your own success, you must first reflect on your current patterns in order to know *what* to change.

Notice that when I say "reflect" on your patterns, I use the term "reflect" as an **action** word. This means that you have to *do* something when you reflect. In this case, I want you to *actively think* about the patterns that you continue to repeat in your life—and to be honest about what makes you do the same things over and over again. This means taking an honest look at things that you do as well as those triggers or the things that cause you to do what you do.

Reflecting on your patterns is the first and most important step because it allows you to understand the foundation or the "reasons" for your actions. Before you can attempt to make any changes, you have to understand and recognize the causes—and patterns of behaviors, relationships, thoughts, emotions and actions within your life that exist--that are directly related to the circumstances that you want to change.

Creators of their success reflect upon patterns in their actions, thoughts and beliefs as a way of understanding their world and determining their place in it, their relationship to it and the actions that they take.

To become a creator of your success, you have to be willing to take a hard look at what has gotten you to this point in your life. You have to be willing to be open and honest **with** yourself **about** yourself. There is no short-cut for this step.

If you don't have a solid, honest base to work from, then everything that you do from this point on will be for nothing. You can't build a solid house on a shaky foundation. Lying to yourself about why you do what you do and not being honest enough to take a hard look at what you do over and over again to create the patterns and circumstances in your life will get you nowhere. It is why people remain victims of their circumstances and why they are trapped within a prison of their own making—existing in a life that they no longer want, but feeling powerless to change it.

Creators of their success in essence create their own power over their lives simply by being honest, open and vulnerable about their habits, their weaknesses and the things that have led them to where they no longer want to be.

It is only through this process that you can create change.

I spent a lot of years in my life repeating the same behaviors and the same way of thinking that kept me in the same position and kept me a victim of the same circumstances over and over again in my life.

Whether it had to do with a health issue, financial situation, relationships or career--every time I just plowed my way through it without thinking and reflecting about WHY I was where I was and thought that I had "overcome" a situation or "gotten past" a problem, I'd find myself smack dab in the middle of the same thing over and over again.

Sometimes things might be better for two weeks, two months or even two years—but as long as I kept *thinking* the same way I kept *doing* the same things—and I kept finding myself in the same circumstances. I called it my own private sense of "deja vu"—that sinking feeling that you've somehow been "here" before.

It wasn't until I was able to take a long, hard look at myself and my habits and tendencies and truly examined my way of thinking that I was able to start making significant changes in my life and turn things around.

> **Note 2 Self: "Only when you are honest with yourself can you begin to change yourself." ~KARS**

Step 2: Redirect your path: Once you have been open and honest with yourself in recognizing and understanding the patterns of actions and thoughts that have led to your circumstances, then you must make a real effort to redirect or change the path that your life is currently taking.

There is a rule of physics that in summary states that an object at rest or in motion will continue at rest or in motion unless acted upon by an outside force. Essentially, what that means is that your life will continue upon its present course unless you act upon it.

In short: You can't just *expect* things to change. You have to *act* in order to *create* change.

But it's not just enough to act. You have to use the information that you gather from examining your patterns of behavior and thoughts to create sound strategies and create a plan of action that will enable you to make the sound decisions necessary for you to take charge of your life.

Creators of their success redirect or adjust their path based on sound information and input from *trusted* sources.

They don't just take what anyone or everyone says as "truth" but instead they look for proof before they accept new information as being the right path for them. They recognize when it is necessary to make changes and have the courage to implement change when it is required.

Too many times we're confronted with the truth about our thoughts, our actions and recognize what needs to be done to make things better—but we just don't act. We keep going along the same path that we've always taken and end up with the same results. (I see you nodding your head on that one because I know you can think of several times when that's happened. ☺)

Don't get me wrong, it's not that we won't *want* things to be different—of course we do! It's just that we don't actively use and apply what we know to be true about ourselves in order to get ourselves on a different path that leads to a different result.

So in order to begin to create success and revise your path, you have to take the information that you've acquired about yourself and the circumstances surrounding you to make changes in your actions so that you can then begin to make changes in the direction that you're traveling along the path of life.

It's like a ripple or domino effect. Once you change one thing, that change affects the next thing, which in turn affects the next and so on and so forth until one day you look up and you've managed to change the direction of the path that you were traveling.

Once you change the direction you're travelling in--then you'll change your outcomes.

Think about it this way. Imagine walking on a beach putting one foot directly in front of the other. As long as you keep placing each foot directly in front of each other on a straight line, you'll keep going straight ahead. But what happens if you place one foot slightly pointed to the left and then pick up with placing the next foot in front of that one—pointed slightly to the left—and the next, and the next? Eventually your path is going to end up going to the left, right?

That's what happens with us in our life's journey. It doesn't take a drastic shift in direction all of the time for us to change course and end up at a different destination. All it takes is a slight alteration applied consistently over time for us to change course and end up in a new place.

> *Note 2 Self: "Sometimes the smallest adjustments are all that's necessary to create the biggest change." ~KARS*

Step 3: Refine your thinking: In order for you to create long-lasting change and to begin to create the success that you want in your life, you MUST change your thinking.

The way of thinking that you had at the time was responsible for the circumstances that you are presently faced with, so it stands to reason that in order for you to being to change your life and create the success that you want, you must begin to think differently—about yourself, about your circumstances, about your abilities, about your future, about your circle of friends and acquaintances, about the way you speak to yourself and about yourself—about everything that you took for granted and took as being "truth".

Creators of their success create new ways of thinking about their world and the ways in which they interact with it. They constantly refine their thinking based on new information instead of dealing with new situations based on old knowledge.

A large part of what causes people to repeat the same mistakes and end up in the same situations time and time again is their mindset and the way they think about the world they live in.

The way that you think about things determines how you interact and respond to situations.

If you're operating with outdated information, then your responses and decisions to new circumstances and situations are going to be based on an old way of thinking.

If you keep responding to new situations using the old way of thinking and doing things, then naturally you're going to get the same old results.

Case in point. Imagine that you're driving along in rush hour traffic and out of nowhere a guy driving a motorcycle jumps in front of you and cuts you off—causing you to slam on your brakes, spill your coffee, send your papers and other items sprawling onto the floor and just narrowly avoid being hit by the car behind you. And to top it off—you're the one getting yelled at by the other drivers because you stopped short. Definitely not a happy moment.

Fast forward five months later when you're driving along in rush hour traffic and you see a completely *different* guy who just happens to be driving a motorcycle on the highway. Your face frowns up a bit; you immediately became agitated and speed up to close the gap between you and the car in front of you and subconsciously grip your coffee a little tighter.

Did motorcycle guy #2 do anything to give you the impression that he was going to jump in front of you? Probably not. You just happened to see him and you went through all of those emotions and subsequently took an action.

If that's the case, then you're operating in the present situation based on old information from a past experience. You did what you did today because you *expected* him to cut you off in traffic based on what had happened *five months ago*. There wasn't any reason for you to believe that he was going to cut you off today (in fact, this was a *completely* different person). But this fact doesn't register with us. What does register is that guys on motorcycles + rush hour traffic = spilled coffee, aggravation and stress. So we act accordingly. We speed up to close the gap so he can't cut us off or we tense up or some people may go as far as to cut *him* off.

The bottom line is that the only connection between this situation and the old situation was your prior experience. Based on this experience, we created an old information database that fueled our way of thinking and shaped our opinions and feelings about guys on motorcycles. This is the information that we use to operate from and ultimately make our decisions and determine our actions.

The key to changing your circumstances and creating success is to approach each new situation with the new information required to deal with it appropriately.

This means that you identify the differences between the old set of circumstances and the current one; gather all of the new information and adjust your way of thinking and approaching a situation prior to taking action.

Let me be clear, *this doesn't mean that you throw away what you've learned from your past experiences.*

Actually, the opposite is true. If you take what you've learned from the past and *combine* that with the new information that you have about the current situation, then you can make wise decisions and plan a sound course of action that fits your present.

In order to move forward, we have to be able to adjust our ways of thinking as necessary to insure that we're making the best decisions possible.

> **Note 2 Self: "The mind is the greatest agent of change." ~KARS**

Step 4: Rejuvenate your spirit: Along the journey, it is necessary for you to take the opportunity to recharge and rejuvenate your spirit. Life has its ups and downs and because you are constantly pouring out and giving of yourself throughout this process, it is necessary--and mandatory--for you to seek out those ways in which you are able to rejuvenate, replenish and restore yourself. This is absolutely necessary, but unfortunately, it is the step that is most neglected.

A large part of what causes people to become victims--and remain victims—of their circumstances—is succumbing to being worn out or "tired" of dealing with "life".

Creators of their success understand that it is necessary for them to seek out ways to rejuvenate their spirit on a regular basis so that they can find joy in living that extends beyond the everyday circumstances that surround them and encompass their lives.

I know what you're thinking—"I've got too much going on; I don't have time for vacations!"

Rejuvenating your spirit doesn't mean you have to take a vacation or get away physically. Those things are nice and it would be great if you would make it a priority to do them on a regular basis.

Rejuvenating your spirit means that you take some time to spend time with yourself—quiet, peaceful, reflective time—where you can truly connect with yourself—so you can recharge.

Keep in mind, this is NOT naptime or time for you to catch up on your sleep and recharge your body. You need that time too, (and have to make sure that you take it), but you have to recharge and refuel mentally and spiritually in order for you to function optimally physically.

We go through life spending time with other people all of the time—at work, events, family functions, social gatherings—even on social media; but we rarely spend quiet, quality time alone with ourselves.

For many people, the definition of "quiet time" is when we turn off the television right before going to sleep and our mind races and all of these thoughts (many of them negative) that seem to overload our brain. That's the time when we worry obsessively about our circumstances and try to figure out our next steps.

"Quiet time" in this scenario isn't about rejuvenation, refueling or anything positive—it's something to be avoided—and so we do—at all costs.

When I talk about taking "quiet time" and rejuvenating your spirit, however, I'm talking about something entirely different.

I'm talking about taking some time to quiet all of the voices in your head; drown out the distractions and spend some time pouring positivity into your mind and spirit.

I'm talking about setting aside time to watch the sunrise or sunset; breathing in all that is good about you; breathing out the negativity that surrounds you; recognizing all the good that is within you and celebrating all the wonderful things about you.

I'm talking about devoting 15 minutes, four times a day to just being good to yourself.

I'm talking about rebuilding that part of you that daily life "happenings" tend to wear down and tear down.

I'm talking about taking some time to reflect on what's great in your life and to think in positive, constructive ways about the things that you can—and will—take steps to change.

Rejuvenating your spirit means that you are taking the time to take care of the essence of YOU.

Notice I said your "essence"—that spiritual part that makes you who you are. It goes beyond what you think to what it is about you that makes you think, say and do what you do. It's understanding, acknowledging and accepting all of the things that make you the person that you are. It's taking the time to engage in the "little" things that make your soul smile.

> *Note 2 Self: "Taking care of my spirit by showing love to my soul is the highest form of self-love."*
> *~KARS*

Step 5: Release yourself to act: I know many of you may be thinking "Why do I have to "release" myself to ACT? I already want things to be different!" Believe it or not, *wanting* things to be different is not enough. Not being happy with the way that your life is going or with the current circumstances doesn't actually *do* anything to change the circumstances of your life or create your success.

Even if you don't want things to be as they are—even if you are sick and tired of being sick and tired of the way things have always been—NOTHING is going to change or be ANY different unless you give yourself permission and RELEASE YOURSELF to act so that you can actually MAKE things different.

We're always seeking permission, validation and acceptance—from our family, friends, professional colleagues, even people we just meet. That's the nature of who we are as human beings.

We ask for it in different ways—from asking outright if what we're doing is okay, to reading into what people say—or don't say—about what we do and coming up with our own conclusions as to whether we need to make some changes or whether our actions are "okay".

The one person that we usually fail to get permission from, however, is us.

While we're so busy looking for validation and acceptance that our actions—and therefore we—are valid from everyone else; we fail to consult the one person who is perhaps the most important in all of this—us—and more personally--YOU.

That means that you have to give yourself **permission and release yourself to take action** to pursue a new job; open yourself up to a new relationship; go back to school; be open to risk or to be vulnerable again.

This may mean looking yourself in the mirror and actually saying out loud "I release myself to..." and stating your next course of action.

It means that you are showing confidence in your ability to act on your own behalf.

Creators of their success understand that action is a required part of the process and give themselves permission to act in ways that will provide long-lasting change in their lives.

By giving yourself permission and releasing yourself to act in ways that are in your best interest, you can take back the power that you have given up by allowing yourself to remain a victim of your circumstances.

By releasing yourself to act, you are serving notice that you will not just sit back and take what comes.

By releasing yourself to act, you are reclaiming your power to control your future.

By releasing yourself to act, you are telling yourself that you not only want things to be different, but you are willing to take responsibility for the actions that are required to make them different.

By releasing yourself to act, you are declaring to yourself that you refuse to remain stuck and that you are ultimately taking control.

By releasing yourself to act, you are committing to making your own decisions and honoring those decisions with action.

By releasing yourself to act, you are recognizing and accepting that you may make mistakes, but you understand and embrace the process because you understand that mistakes are a part of life.

> *Note 2 Self: "We can always do whatever we wish—we just have to let ourselves go do it."*
> *~KARS*

It is important for you to recognize that all aspects of this five-step process of change are necessary as you both begin the process and continue the process of creating the success that you want in your life.

Long-lasting change does not occur and is not *sustained* without ensuring that you are addressing all of these areas, and it requires that you are completely honest with yourself throughout this process.

We had to begin with an examination of the process of change so that you would understand at a glance the journey that lies ahead, now it is time to examine exactly what it is that we're trying so hard to achieve.

What is Success?

When I ask you the question, "What is success?" what immediately comes you mind?

Most people provide answers that have something to do with material possessions—nice cars, large homes, a certain amount of money in the bank, a steady job—or having a certain status level or career.

Rarely, if ever, is success equated with things that are internal or things that cannot be taken away by disasters or a change in your circumstances—loss of a job, change in the market, etc.

One of the key things that we have to understand first and foremost before we go any further, is that while material things represent acquisitions within our circumstances—they are not in and of themselves, a definition of our level of success.

> *Note 2 Self: Success is a personal definition that we mistake for a public demonstration. ~KARS*

In reality, the answer to the question, "What is success?" is in fact a much more personal definition that is more internal than external and that is more so based on the things within your life that bring you joy, happiness and fulfillment.

When thinking about success in light of what makes us most happy and fulfilled, the definition of success can be said to consist of three areas:

1) fueling your passion;
2) aligning with your purpose; and
3) building your legacy.

When we *really* think about it—our dissatisfaction with our circumstances and the way that our lives are at the current time usually come down to a longing for more--wanting something that makes us feel "alive" and energized (passion); makes us feel as if we were created for a reason (purpose), and leaves some tangible proof that we existed when it's all said and done (legacy). The other material things that we achieve are bonus items that come as a *result* of us being happy, satisfied and fulfilled—not the other way around.

The problem arises when we mistakenly turn our focus on the material things—which in fact are the public demonstrations of the accepted definition or representation of "success"-- instead of focusing our energies on achieving and creating our personal definition of success.

When we do this, we end up being caught in a cycle of chasing "things" rather than living a life of substance, which leads to feelings of victimization, dissatisfaction and unhappiness.

Changing your definition of success is a crucial step in the process. Once you understand that identifying and pursuing a life based on what fuels your passion; aligns with your purpose and builds your legacy will allow you to create the success that you crave and enable you to stop being a victim of your circumstances, take control of your life and start creating the life you were destined to live—then you are well on your way.

Change your thinking and your focus; change your life.

Unless you accept this fundamental shift in your thinking, then there is no need to move any further.

Creators of their success understand that it is not the pursuit of material things that can be taken away that constitute success—but rather the creation of a life filled with passion, purpose and the desire to leave a legacy that enables them to find the drive necessary to create the life that they desire to live.

Creators vs Victims

You've picked up this book because you want to change your life from being one marked by being a victim of your circumstances, to one where you are the creator and driver of your own success. In order to do that, we need to understand the differences between "creators" and "victims".

Fundamentally, there are some distinctive characteristics that define and differentiate Creators and Victims. (If you've noticed, I've already started outlining some of them in the first parts of this book.)

Understanding these distinctions can assist you in determining what you need to do differently in order to recognize the patterns that have kept you from moving on and making changes in your life up until now. This is not an exhaustive list by any means, but serves to provide an overview for comparison purposes.

> *Note 2 Self: Your success has more to do with who you are internally than what you have externally.*
> *~KARS*

Being the creator of your success—NOT a victim of your circumstances requires a fundamental shift in your mindset and the foundation of your very core. With that being said, once you truly understand and accept the shift, the process of change begins immediately.

Creators: Fundamentally, being a Creator means that you are in control.

You do the acting upon your environment instead of waiting to react to things that happen.

You make the decisions about what happens, when and why instead of selecting from a set of choices that others have set before you. Making decisions means that you have a fundamental understanding of the consequences and results that come with the decisions to be made and you take full responsibility for them.

Creators are leaders who take responsibility for their actions and the actions of others in their charge. They are not afraid of being the ones who will step up if the need arises to assume responsibility and will express their opinion when called upon. Creators consider input from others, although they ultimately make their own decisions and draw their own conclusions.

Creators manage their time and rhythm and flow well and have a command and understanding of their work habits and internal "clock". They are not swayed and controlled by others' concept of time and require that others respect and value their time.

Creators may not be in an ideal situation, but they recognize that they have the ability to change their circumstances and do not let a temporary condition affect their permanent plans or self-image.

Victims: Victims, on the other hand, do not exhibit control over their environment or their lives for the most part. They are constantly reacting to things that happen to them—usually the same things over and over again—and are constantly making excuses as to why things are not working out as they'd hoped.

Victims rarely take charge in situations, preferring to follow others instead of stepping forward to lead. They allow others to influence their decisions and make choices based on selections that others place before them instead of creating their own unique decisions based on their own knowledge and input.

Victims have a poor sense of time and frequently feel overwhelmed, tired and overworked. They feel as if they have no control in their lives and frequently feel as if they have "no choice" in their lives being the way it is.

Victims frequently talk about not "wanting" their lives to be as they are, but when pressed to take some different form of action to change, will find excuses not to do anything.

You cannot be a creator of your success if you are a victim of your circumstances. The two cannot exist at the same time.

When you understand that the things that happen in your life are within your control, then you can begin the process of changing things and creating the life that you ultimately want and are destined to live. Take a good hard look at yourself. Examine your patterns of who you are, and then let's look at what's holding you back.

2. THE BOOGEYMAN DOESN'T LIVE HERE ANYMORE

Evicting The Element of Fear

Our decision-making ability is rooted in our belief systems and the way in which we see the world and our place in it. Our views of the world are largely rooted in our perceptions—and nothing clouds and shapes our perceptions—and therefore causes more issues when it comes to creating a successful life—than fear.

When we examine all of the aspects of our lives that truly scare us-- those things that frighten us to our core and keep us paralyzed in our current situations, wrapped in our comfort zones of issues and mediocrity--the underlying common thread is a fundamental fear of the unknown.

It's not that we're afraid that we can't do something or that we'll fail at something new--yes, that's part of it too--but it's more that we don't know for CERTAIN that we're going to succeed. Fear of the unknown is in essence fear of the "boogeyman"--that shadowy creature that plagued you when you were a child that lurked under your bed, in your closet or in any dark crevice or corner waiting to pounce out at you once the lights were turned out.

Now you couldn't actually SEE the boogeyman, but that's what made him all the more terrifying. Because you couldn't see him, you couldn't be sure he WASN'T there, now could you?

Evicting the element of fear from your life has more to do with understanding, acknowledging and dealing with fear than it does ignoring or banishing it outright.

Fear is an emotional state that nature provided to us as a means of protecting us from harm. Every creature is naturally programmed with a "flight or fight" response when encountering something new. For many of us, however, the "flight" response took over permanently and we've never developed our "fight" response when it comes to pursuing our passion, purpose, legacy and our personal and professional development.

In this section we'll examine strategies that will help you to identify the "boogeyman" that exists in your life in all its forms; develop sound action steps to address those issues, move past them and transform your "flight" into a "fight" response and effectively evict the element of fear from your life as a hindrance to your path to becoming a creator of your success.

Fear is the number one reason that we don't achieve what want to in our lives.

Fear of failure, what others will say; what others think; rejection, disappointment—and yes, even fear of success!

The other examples of fear you understand, but I know, I know—you're probably thinking—"Success is what I'm working for. I would NEVER be afraid of succeeding!". But it's true!

Imagine this scenario:

You've been working day and night to climb your way up the ladder in a company where you started in an entry-level position—maybe working in the mailroom. As you worked harder and learned more, you were promoted and moved up. With each promotion you were given more responsibility. Now here it is a few years later and you're offered a position that would make you the youngest Vice-President in the company and have you presiding over the department where you were first hired as a mail clerk. You'd think you'd be ecstatic, right?

Well, now you start thinking about the people who were once all your "bosses" who are now going to be your "colleagues"—all the other members of the senior management team who at every opportunity tell stories about how they remember when you first started working in the mail room—and how young you were--and still are. So now you start second-guessing yourself and your abilities because you're also the only one at the senior management level without a college degree. Thoughts of "Can I do this?" "What do they really think of me?" and "Am I really prepared for this?" start crowding your mind.

So what do you do? You start to subconsciously self-sabotage. Or you turn down the promotion. Anything not to have to subject yourself to the doubts and fears. That's the definition of the fear of success.

The key to overcoming fear is not to ignore it, but instead to face it, understand it—and yes, to **use** it!

~ *Fears are the stories we tell ourselves.* ~

When we experience fear, we are telling ourselves stories about our perception of reality—or our version of reality. So what we need to do is to recognize just what is developing this perception and use it to create the elements that will help us to develop our success instead of serving to keep us as victims of our circumstances.

The Truth About Fear:

1. Fear is emotional.

The main factor that we forget when dealing with fear is that while it's true we experience an incredibly overwhelming physical response when afraid--our hearts race, our palms sweat, our legs shake--fear is actually only an emotion--and emotions come and go.

That means it's only temporary. Therefore, it stands to reason, that if you can gain control over your emotions, you can gain control over your fear.

So in order for us to begin to evict the element of fear from our lives, the first step is to understand and recognize that the fear that we are experiencing is an emotional response to a trigger, and as a result, we should understand that this will indeed—pass.

Creators of their success don't make permanent decisions based on temporary emotions.

2. We fear things we don't understand.

When it really comes right down to it, we fear things that we don't understand all that well because it's so much easier for our minds to "fill in the blanks" and create the rest of the story than it is for us to discover the truth.

The best way to address this is to actually identify the reasons why you're afraid and list all of them. Be as reasonable as possible in explaining an answer to each one. The key in this case is to build an understanding in order to get past your fear. If it's a person or a culture or a way of life or a new place, then list the reasons why you're afraid and then do your research to address those concerns. Don't just let your fears and lack of understanding continue.

Creators of their success seek to identify the things that they don't understand and to ask the questions necessary to obtain the knowledge and information they need to overcome their fear.

3. *We fear the unknown.*

When we encounter new situations and experiences, it is natural for us to want to pull back because of our fear because we're not sure of what's going to happen—Will it go well? Will it go badly? Will it be successful? Will I get hurt (again)?

Sometimes we don't know *what* we're afraid of exactly—we just know that we're afraid—so we pull back and we run—or worse yet, we stand still and we go nowhere.

The way to address this is two-fold, first—identify exactly what it is that you're afraid of.

Give your fears a name. If you can name it, then you can conquer it.

It's so much easier to remain fearful of something when you don't know what it is.

If you can't conceptualize it, quantify it, explain it, identify it, or wrap your head around it—naturally you fear it.

I'm a big fan of animated movies (okay, I'm a fanatic ☺) and I particularly love the DreamWorks movie "Over The Hedge". It's about a group of small woodland creatures who awake from hibernation one spring to discover that their habitat has been all but obliterated and replaced with a sprawling suburban development. All that's left of the woods they once knew is a square of "green space" surrounded by an enormous hedge.

Well, of course, they've never seen a hedge, don't know what to call it and since it seems to go on forever, they don't know what to make of it and are naturally afraid of it. While they're huddled together in a group staring up at this overbearing monstrosity that looms above them, they repeatedly ask each other what it is. Hammie the Squirrel offers this suggestion: "Can we call it Steve? I'd be much less afraid of it if I just knew what it was and Steve seems like a nice name."

Now I'm not saying that you have to call your fears pet names like "Steve", (but hey, if it works, do it ☺) but what I **am** saying is that when you identify specifically what it is that you're afraid of, then you have something tangible to direct your efforts towards and you can come up with a strategy and a plan of action to enable you to overcome it.

Secondly, your additional fear comes from feeling that you can't deal with the outcomes of the situation, so you need to identify two things: the best-case scenario and the worst-case scenario.

Identify the worst-case scenario so you can be prepared for emergencies. List what could happen; how you would deal with it, and then put it aside. Don't dwell on it incessantly and work yourself up worrying about it. Just list the top three worst case outcomes and create your plan to deal with each one and leave it at that. Just knowing that you're prepared helps a lot.

You then identify the best-case scenario of what can go right and focus on that as your Vision of Success Mind Movie to calm you, encourage you and direct your energy in a positive direction. In this way, you become solution-oriented instead of problem-led. When you are solution-oriented, you feel more in control, which makes you feel better and lessens your fear.

Creators of their success have a positive image of themselves being successful to aspire to in their actions.

3. THE MESSAGE IN THE MIRROR

Self-Talk & The Power of Language

The words that you use to describe yourself and the things that you say to yourself tell a great deal about whether you are a creator of your success or a victim of your circumstances.

> ***Note 2 Self:** What others say about you doesn't matter as much as what you say about yourself.*
> *~KARS*

The language that you use with yourself determines your mood, your approach, how you deal with things, and ultimately how successful you are during the course of your day and as a result, your life.

Try this exercise. Say these two sentences out loud and pay attention to how you feel after saying each one.

1.) I *am* tired. I *am* overwhelmed.

How did you feel when you said each sentence? What came to mind?

Now say these two sentences out loud.

2) I *feel* tired. I *feel* overwhelmed.

How did you feel when you said the second set of sentences? What came to mind?

Notice any difference?

When you said the first set of sentences, you talked about who you "are" because you described a permanent state (I AM). This is how we usually talk to ourselves and about ourselves as individuals when what we're really supposed to be doing is describing our feelings—which are temporary.

When you said the second set of sentences, you used the proper wording by saying you "feel" a certain way and described a set of emotions, which is a **temporary** state.

Far too often we cross our signals of communication—with ourselves—and describe temporary emotions using permanent words. This leads us to feel more hopeless and more despondent than we need to for the simple fact that we don't recognize from our language that this is just a passing state and that it will get better.

Believe it or not, the way that we talk to ourselves has a lot to do with our notions of how capable and confident we feel about ourselves and our ability to be successful and create the lives that we want. When you exhibit positive self-talk, you enhance your ability to carry out the vision that you have for your life.

Just as positive self-talk enhances your ability to be a creator of your success, the opposite holds true. People who exhibit negative self-talk—or who don't engage in self-talk at all—are more likely to be victims of their circumstances. As humans, we thrive on communication—and we are constantly looking for affirmations of our worth, abilities and capabilities.

> **Note 2 Self: Sometimes what is not said speaks louder than what is heard. ~KARS**

When we DON'T say out loud that we are capable, worthy, talented—or any of the other myriad of positive things that can be used to describe us—but instead focus on all of the negative things that we use day in and day out; we rob ourselves of the positive reinforcement that we need to thrive.

It goes beyond simply having a "good attitude" about yourself or your day. The way you talk about yourself and your life determines how you live your life. The more negative things that you have to say every day, the more of a negative view of life that you have and the more of a victim's mentality that you exhibit.

> **Note 2 Self: When you think about the way you describe your day, that determines the way you live your life.**
>
> **Life is not meant to be "endured", "overcome", "gotten through", or "tolerated". It is to be cherished, enjoyed, shared, loved, and above all, LIVED. ~KARS**

What are your self-talk habits?

Think about all of the ways that you describe yourself.

What are the words that you use to speak directly to yourself during the day?

How do you encourage yourself when you find yourself in a difficult situation?

What do you say to comfort yourself when you are afraid?

You are the only person who is actually *with* you 24 hours a day. The way that you talk to yourself should be an indicator of how others should speak to you.

If used properly, self-talk and the effective use of language is a powerful tool to create your success. When I was lying in that hospital bed, I talked to myself over and over again to get through the painful injections and procedures that I had to endure on my road to recovery. During the times when I felt like giving up and giving in, I urged myself to push forward and do just one more thing by talking to myself out loud. I was my biggest cheerleader during the days when I didn't feel my best, but needed to muster the motivation to give it another try on yet another day at building my business.

Creators of their success use positive self-talk as a tool to motivate themselves, encourage themselves and keep themselves going along their journey.

As you begin this process, understand that you can become your best asset, but you can also become your own worst enemy. Self-talk in your darkest hour can plunge you back into a victim's mentality and can cause you to beat up on yourself when things aren't going your way. The important thing to remember is that when and if this happens, you need to recognize it and correct it as soon as possible.

Create a recording of positive self-talk sayings that you can play for yourself; have an accountability partner that you can call to give you a "positive pep talk" or just to "tell you something good" and you can even keep a journal or post-it list of positive thoughts and affirmations that you can read several times a day.

Something as simple as taking five minutes several times a day to focus on reading, saying and reinforcing positive thoughts and messages to yourself can do wonders in creating the right mindset and assist you in sustaining long-term success in your life.

There are countless strategies and action steps that you can implement. The key is to be consistent and to recognize when there are too many negative messages coming in so you can take the appropriate action to correct it and redirect the flow.

4. DECONSTRUCT TO RECONSTRUCT

Dissecting the Vision: Laying the Path

> *Note 2 Self: It is impossible to know where you want to go unless you first have a VISION of your destination. ~KARS*

So we've talked about the changes needed in your thinking. We've identified the five-step process of change. We've looked at the difference between being a creator versus a victim. We've identified what it means to have positive self-talk and the power of language in the creation of success and we've talked about what it means to be successful.

Now we need to figure out—how do we do it exactly? What's the plan? What are the specific steps that we take? Where do we go from here?

Perhaps the thing that most people want to know is this—how do I get from my current circumstances to create the success that I want for my life?

That is the single question that more than anything *keeps* people in the same condition, year after year and creates a situation where they become frustrated and feel overwhelmed because they don't feel as if they're making any progress.

In this chapter we're going to outline a step-by-step strategy for identifying your vision of success and walk you through the process of how to use it to create a solid action plan that you can follow to achieve it.

Vision Boards vs Mind Movies

Vision Boards: Most of you have probably heard of Vision Boards—where you cut out pictures of the things that you want that represent your idea or vision of your future success (usually material things like a house, car, boat, jewelry, travel destination, photo of a career, etc.) and paste them onto a poster board, label the items and then hang the board in a prominent place for you to refer to throughout the year. The idea is that you should use the Vision Board as a motivational tool to remind you of the goals that you're working towards.

Vision Boards are usually created at the beginning of the year and many people and organizations have begun having "Vision Board Parties" where they get together as a group to create and share their Vision Boards. The issue with Vision Boards is that they are static, representations of someone else's visuals for your goals (i.e., you have to use the picture of the house or car that's close to the one that you want if the exact one isn't available). As a result, the "vision" that you are creating isn't completely accurate in terms of being a true representation of the picture you have in your mind, and most times you're using material possessions to define success.

What's more, Vision Boards don't have a way of conveying your feelings and emotions through the photos. You can add short phrases or words if you like, but the majority of the board is meant to be comprised of photos.

Mind Movies: Mind Movies on the other hand, are more comprehensive. What makes a Mind Movie distinctive is that you actually get to use your imagination and picture yourself being successful.

In a Mind Movie, you are creating an actual narrative of your vision of success—with YOU as the star.

Mind Movies require you to actually *imagine* yourself being successful. You need to envision all of the aspects of it—the sounds, the sights, the tastes, the smells. You need to picture what you'd be wearing; where you would work; what you'd be driving; who you would be working with; etc.

Success isn't one-dimensional. It encompasses all of our senses, so it stands to reason that our vision of success and what our lives would be like if we were to find that thing that enabled us to fuel our passion; align with our purpose and build our legacy would be multi-sensory and multi-faceted.

The more senses we can engage when we create our Mind Movie, the more of a connection we have to our future success—and therefore, the more dedication we will have to achieving it.

KARS Released & Ready™ Mind Movie Process

Whereas Vision Boards end with the simple application of pictures to a blank board, the KARS Released & Ready™ Mind Movie process has four main steps:

1) Visualization of the Mind Movie of Success
2) Recording the Mind Movie Script.
3) KARS Deconstruct to Reconstruct™ Process
4) Laying the Path: Action Planning

Visualization: Visualization is a powerful tool and we use it in the creation of a Mind Movie to have you actually close your eyes, use your imagination and picture a day in the life of you living your dream. Be as detailed as possible—right down to the clothes that you're wearing and what you have for lunch. The idea is to capture everything—sights, sounds, tastes, smells, emotions, textures, temperatures, décor, furnishings—anything and everything that provides a complete and total picture of you and your dream in living, breathing, action. It's as if you were being followed by a camera crew for the day and they recorded you and you used that recording to transcribe your events and create a script for a Mind Movie about your future day of success—your Vision.

Mind Movie Script: In recording the Mind Movie Script, it is important for you to be as detailed as possible when recording your vision, so you can capture all of the elements that you created in your mind's eye. These details will be very important when you are extracting information to create the action plan. The best way to record the Script is to write it in the form of a narrative, just as if you were writing a novel where the scene and setting information was important to the story.

You should also record your actions for the day—any meetings, locations, modes of transportation, leisure activities, responsibilities, people you interacted with and their roles, etc. Keep in mind that is an opportunity for you to let your imagination run wild, so feel free to imagine and record conversations and describe your clothing, appearance, feelings, thoughts, etc.

The entire point is to capture the day from an observer's point of view but with insight into your thoughts and feelings—taking care to record everything with as much detail as possible.

Deconstruct to Reconstruct: The key to the KARS Released & Ready™ Mind Movie Process is the Deconstruct to Reconstruct Process. After you have created the Mind Movie Script, you will use this to pull out the information that you need for your strategy plan and lay out your path for success.

The Deconstruct to Reconstruct Process calls for you to examine each area of your Mind Movie Script in turn and work backwards (hence the Deconstruction)—by asking yourself the question "What is needed to make that happen?"---and then writing down the answer.

Keep in mind that at this point, you're not overly concerned about *how* you're going to actually *make* it happen (i.e., where you're going to get the funding, materials, resources, personnel, etc.), the only thing that you're interested in is *what* is needed.

The reason we're doing this, is to develop a working outline of what it takes to create your Vision of Success. Call it a "Scaffold". This is just for us to be able to have a rough idea—or framework of what's needed.

You keep going backwards through each section of the Mind Movie Script, asking yourself the same question and recording your response until you work your way all the way back to the beginning. Because you worked backwards (asking your question in reverse order), once you've completed the Deconstruction process, you'll have a rough order or plan of what needs to be done to create your Mind Movie Script if you were to go forwards down your list. Mind Movies work for personal as well as professional Visions of Success.

Here's an example.

Let's say my Personal Mind Movie Script was a snapshot of a person rebuilding after having successfully purchased their first home.

Script:

> *As I pull into driveway in front of the two-car garage, I can hardly contain my excitement. To be finally standing in front of my very own two story brick town-home is like a dream come true! I'm elated and have a huge smile on my face as I walk up the five steps to the front porch—my front porch, I think with a smile—open the screen door and insert the key that the realtor had just placed in my hand at the closing just that morning. It had been a long road, but I had managed to purchase my first home with little money down after working hard within a credit repair program. As I pushed open the front door, I couldn't help but smile as I envisioned where I would place the new furniture that I had saved to buy and that would be delivered later that afternoon.*

Deconstruction List: Based on the Mind Movie Script above, the Deconstruction list would look something like this:

> *What is needed to make this happen?*
> - *Two-story brick townhome with 2-car garage & front porch*
> - *Down payment (small)*
> - *Credit repair program*
> - *Realtor*
> - *New furniture*
> - *Savings account (furniture)*
> - *Car*

Voila`!

You now have a checklist of items to focus on for the Laying the Path: Action Planning Phase.

Using a Mind Movie, the Script and the Deconstruction process means that there are no wasted efforts. You're not focusing on anything that's not directly related to your Mind Movie/Vision for Success.

Laying the Path/Action Plan: Now based on the Deconstruction list, I can then begin creating the items for my Laying the Path: Action Plan. This is a plan that I create where I take the items that are included and schedule them according to what will bring me the most success.

This is when I decide not only what I will work on, but also when I will work on it---taking care to revisit my Mind Movie Script periodically so that I can see myself being successful in what I'm doing.

With that in mind, I take each component from the list and then brainstorm action steps that need to be taken in order to achieve each piece. For example, under "credit repair program" I make a list of additional steps—locate a program; identify the time and costs involved; call to research the steps needed; select a program; enroll in the program; complete the program, etc. Do this for each component of your checklist and then use those items to determine what actions you need to take in order to achieve your goals.

Keep in mind that you don't need a lot of time—15 minutes a day is enough to get you started so you can make progress over time.

> *Note 2 Self: Start each journey (day, week, month, year) by visualizing yourself being successful in the things that you want to do, then make a realistic action plan to achieve that success.*
> *~KARS*

This process also requires you to create an overall timeline for the achievement of your success goals (five years, ten years, etc.) and then work backwards to insure that you are allowing yourself enough time to work on each goal.

This will require some research to determine how much time is actually needed at minimum so that you can plan effectively and create goals that are realistic based on your access to resources, time, etc. at each phase. For example, if one of your goals is to purchase a house and you don't have any savings, your credit rating is sub-par and you don't have any income, then it's not realistic for you to be able to buy a $300,000 home in two months.

The point is to be realistic, but not become overwhelmed or frustrated by the process. This process is designed to provide you with an action guide of what steps you need to take in order to create your success so that you can leave the days of being a victim of your circumstances behind.

No one said it was going to be easy.

If there were mistakes that had been made in your life that you need to correct, then your journey may take a little longer—but if you are committed to the process, then it can be done successfully.

The key is to integrate your long-term, mid-term and everyday action steps and planning into one overall plan of action so that you're able to see at a glance how everything interconnects and you can measure your progress. Taking the time to write out your Mind Movie Vision of Success and Deconstruct your Action Plan for each facet of your life is key to resetting your frame of reference and changing your underlying foundation from a victim's mentality to a creator's mentality.

You also need to record the things that you HAVE done along the journey. Too often we have these long "to do" lists of things that have to be done, but rarely do we record the things that we HAVE done—and are able to celebrate.

The process of change requires celebration in order to maintain motivation.

No one wants to continue to do things if they don't feel that they're making progress. Therefore, you have to be able to not only identify those things that you have to do, but also to remember to celebrate what you have done and pat yourself on the back for consistently making strides. Remember, even a little step still takes you away from where you have been.

The strategies and thought processes that have been outlined in this book will need to become a regular part of your day to day lifestyle, but not only that—you'll need to develop a support system and make changes in the types of people that you have in your life in order to ensure your transition from victim to creator.

5. COOPERATION & COLLABORATION

Building the Team You Need

With everything else that you're taking on in tackling this challenge, the issue of examining the type of people that you have in your circle is one that needs to be of utmost importance. Because of the amount of time and effort that is going to be required of you in order to change your life in this way, it is imperative that you create a support system that is built upon trust, cooperation and collaboration

What that means is that the friends, neighbors, coworkers or even family members that have had a prominent place in your life will now have to be re-examined. As a creator of your success, you will need to have people in your life who help you to build cooperative and collaborative relationships where both parties benefit, not one-sided relationships where one-party loses.

"Win-Win" vs "Gimme-Gimme"

"Win-Win": "Win-Win" relationships are those that are beneficial to all parties where equal partnerships are formed. They are representative of the true spirit of collaboration where everyone is involved and demonstrates a team spirit where all parties work toward the greater good of the overall partnership. Creators of their own success create win-win relationships.

"Gimme-Gimme": "Gimme-Gimme" relationships are those are not beneficial to all parties and where unequal partnerships are formed. They include more "taking" than giving and there's always a "leader" who tends to benefit more than the other parties. There are a few people who make all of the decisions, so there's little collaboration and there's little or no team spirit.

Forming Relationships

As you work towards creating your success and changing your life, forming new relationships is going to be key. You'll find that implementing the action plans that you've developed, along with finding the support necessary to keep you going will be accomplished through expanding your circle to include new friends and colleagues.

The most important thing to remember is that even though there may be more that needs to be done, *you* don't have to do it all yourself.

> *Note 2 Self: You may not have to do it all yourself, but you have to make sure it gets done. ~KARS*

Victims of their circumstances tend to gravitate towards others who are in similar situations—those who feel hopeless and helpless and who may have difficulty moving beyond their current situation.

They seldom build integrated and expansive teams to support them in their efforts and frequently isolate themselves because they give in to feelings of despair and feel that there is little or no hope for them to make sweeping changes in their lives.

Creators of their success, on the other hand, create new relationships and partnerships with those who are more advanced than they are and are willing to learn from others so that they may become better and improve their lives. Creators understand that it is important to expand their network if they are to increase their net worth. They focus on building a team to assist and support them in their efforts and recognize that different people fill different roles in their lives.

The main difference between the two is comfort. Creators of their success are willing to shed their comfort level to take risks and expand their circle to include other people—different kinds of people—than they may have previously been comfortable interacting with or had experience with because they understand that being uncomfortable is the key to growth and growth means that their situations and circumstances will change and improve for the better.

So ask yourself an honest question. What type of person are you when it comes to your relationships?

How comfortable have you been in the circles that you have established?

How willing are you to form new relationships and strike out to create "win-win" partnerships and establish new networks?

You cannot be committed to being a creator of your success without a proven network that includes collaborating with people who are better than you are—period.

There is no way for you to become better without pushing yourself beyond your current boundaries when it comes to relationships and your interactions with other people.

Let's face it. Forming new networks and learning how to collaborate with others is a somewhat scary proposition—especially for someone who has never had to do it before. But unless you are willing to do it consistently and work at building those relationships over time, then you will have a difficult time growing beyond a certain level.

This is more than just about getting things done—this is about expanding your knowledge base and learning more about the way that the world works. There are some things you can acquire by accessing static information, that's true. But there are other things that you can really only gain by communicating with other people who have actually gained expertise in an area.

The key is to determine what types of people you need to have on your team and in your circle and then to actively seek out forming positive relationships with those people. Be diligent in your search and understand that not everyone you meet is going to be a match or fit with you personally, so be open to the process and keep expanding your network so that your constantly adding new people.

Cross-check your action plan and review your Mind Movie to identify the types of people who are mentioned within your script. Then make a list of where you might be able to attend networking functions, facilitate introductions or observe those types of groups interacting, collaborating and working together.

If this is your first attempt at expanding your network and building new relationships outside of your normal circles, you'll need to learn the social cues and ways of communicating that exist within the new groups that you're entering.

Don't rush things and don't force yourself on others. Building relationships takes time and establishing a rapport and relationship is a process. Be honest about what you're looking for and what you bring to the table. Determine what you need and what you have to offer in the #win-win by examining your action plan.

That doesn't mean that every time you meet someone new you're "all business". Quite the opposite. Most relationships are based upon a mutual understanding and the development of a connection that goes beyond the negotiated #win-win, so don't be afraid to show people who you are personally. Strike a balance and understand the setting so that you can respond appropriately.

Role Play

When you do begin to develop new relationships, understand that the people who have been a part of your life before you began this journey may feel left out. That's completely understandable. It's up to you to decide what role they will play—if any—in your new life.

Understand that people can play different roles in your life than they may have held in the past and that it's completely up to you to decide if and how they travel with you on this journey.

The important thing to do is to communicate your needs and be honest about your decisions and their roles so that there are no misunderstandings about the place that they hold in your life. Just because someone is no longer your best friend doesn't mean that person can no longer be a friend. There are some relationships that you may decide you are better off without, some that you deem worth saving and some you want to change a bit—the role that they play completely up to you.

6. REFLECTION, REDIRECTION & RELEASE

Making Decisions, Taking Action

> *Note 2 Self: When you have made a DECISION--not a "choice", a "wish" or a "want"--for your life, things will become different once you have started the process to make them different. ~KARS*

There comes a point in your life when you have to make a decision.

Not a choice.

But a decision.

This is one of those times.

A choice is a selection that you make from various options that are presented to you by other people. You usually don't necessarily assume responsibility for the consequences of choices. Most times you don't even think about the consequences that occur as a result of a choice, because, well—it wasn't really *up* to you. You were almost forced into it since you only had these particular options to select from.

A decision on the other hand, is different.

A decision is entered into fully aware and completely knowledgeable of the consequences. You know *exactly* what you're getting yourself into, what it means and what's required.

What's the biggest difference between choices and decisions?

When you make a choice, you're not especially obligated to follow through on it because you really didn't want to make the selection to begin with—so you're not completely invested.

But when you make a decision—you're obligated to follow it up and *honor it* with some type of action because, well, you *know better*--- and decisions must be honored by actions.

So here we are.

You've come to the part of the book where we talk about what it means to make decisions and take actions based on determining your course for your life. Everything that we've talked about up until now has all been great—in theory.

But fundamentally, unless you have an understanding—and a commitment—to making sound decisions for your life—not expressing wants, or desires or things that you *wish* or would *like* to happen—but actually *making* and *acting* upon the decisions that will change your life—then nothing about your life will be different. It's that simple.

Reflection

At the beginning of the book, you were introduced to the five step process of change. And the very first step required you to reflect on your patterns.

Reflection is a major requirement in the process of making sound decisions because within the process of reflecting, you take the necessary time to examine the different variables and variances and all of the consequences and any other elements that have to go into the equation *before* you make your final decision.

There is actually a process to reflecting. It doesn't mean just taking a few moments to think about something. To reflect on a decision and consider all of the consequences and possible outcomes means that you refocus your mind away from distractions to actually think through the different possibilities before you arrive at a final determination of what course of action you're going to take.

It means that you actually take some time *away*—where you can remove yourself from the situation if possible—and give yourself time to go through the different options

Redirection

Sometimes the most difficult thing is to *know* that you need to do things differently, but for some reason, you can't bring yourself to make the changes necessary to bring about the new outcomes that you want.

The power of Redirection is in taking an honest look at who you are and what your tendencies have been—and to redirect or change your actions so that you're able to change the path being traveled and therefore change your destination.

Going through this process does you absolutely no good if you don't make a commitment to redirecting your thoughts, decision-making and ultimately your actions.

Redirection doesn't mean that you've been a horrible person who has done nothing but fail. It doesn't mean that you beat yourself up or berate yourself for any mistakes that you may have made in the past. It doesn't mean that you are somehow not "enough" because you made a decision to change.

Redirection instead means that you are strong enough, self-aware enough and confident enough in yourself and your abilities to take responsibility for your life, your journey and your future to make the adjustments necessary for growth and progress.

It has been often-quoted that "the definition of insanity is doing the same thing over and over again, but expecting a different result".

Well, the purpose of Redirection is having the strength of mind and resilience of spirit to not only recognize the changes that need to be made (after careful reflection) but to take the necessary action to apply your new information in order to create applied knowledge and create a new model of success.

> *Note 2 Self: It doesn't matter how many "tools" you have; if you don't use them, nothing gets built. ~KARS*

Release

I hear people all the time who say they "want" things to be different, but they don't understand why they just can't seem to pull the trigger, take the plunge and take that first step to truly redirecting the path that their life's journey is taking. So often they seem to be "stuck" for some reason and as a result, they keep repeating the same cycle of being a victim in so many different aspects of their lives.

The question they keep asking themselves is "why" they choose to remain in the same place and the same state even though they know better.

The answer in a lot of cases is very simple—Release.

The concept of Release involves letting go. Letting go of your past. Letting go of your fear. Letting go of the myriad and multitude of reasons that you constantly conjure up whenever it's time to take a step in a new direction.

Release involves giving yourself permission to want more and to be better. It means that once you have been honest and vulnerable to reflect fully upon your circumstances, situations, rationales and fundamental reasons for why things are and have been, that you are willing to redirect your path so that you can achieve more, and then finally to actually *allow* yourself to experience your new state and way of being and doing.

You can't move forward if you're constantly dragging the old baggage of disappointments, self-doubt, experiences, failures and the way things were into your future. You have to release it all—the emotions, the pain, the struggle and yes, even the personal connections and relationships if necessary.

Release gives you the power to command a new beginning.

It's not hiding from your past, but instead requires you to face it in order to learn from it and grow because of it.

Effectively practicing the art of Reflection, Redirection and Release requires commitment. It requires honesty. It requires vulnerability and most of all it requires strength. Accepting this process is perhaps the most important aspect of making the fundamental change from being a victim of your circumstances to becoming a creator of your success.

When you take the time and make the effort to take an honest assessment and review of your life, determine the adjustments that need to be made as a result and then let everything go that doesn't serve your best interests for growth and give yourself permission to act on your own behalf—you are not just taking responsibility for your life, but you are living your life boldly instead of having life happen *to* you.

This process takes practice, yes. But it's most definitely worth it if you want to have the life that you know deep within that you are destined to have. You can't get to where you want to go if you're not willing to make the sacrifices and the changes.

This book isn't about creating motivational sayings and giving you short sound bites. This book is about creating an opportunity for you to not only gain the information that you need to truly understand the fundamental aspects of your life that need to be present in order to insure your success—but it also outlines the steps that you must take in order to apply the information and strategies to make your Mind Movie of Success become a reality.

So, with all that you've read and explored thus far—of course you're wondering, what's next?

7. 12 STEPS

Creating the Life You Were Destined To Live

> *Note 2 Self: When you truly believe that you deserve the best life has to offer, you will stop at nothing to get it.*

I've provided a great deal of information and taken the time to present the fundamental differences between what constitutes being a victim and creating your own success. I've laid out steps, activities and presented examples for you to use in thinking about your own life.

Now it's time for implementation.

Creating the life that you were destined to live comes down to taking twelve steps. You can take these steps over the course of days, weeks or months—the timeframe is up to you.

What is required is dedication.

You have to fundamentally not only *want* to make the changes and experience the growth and progress, but you have to actually do the work to get it and achieve your outcomes and make that vision of success in your mind a reality.

Before you begin, you need to understand that this process is a journey and that you can apply the concepts presented in this book to different aspects of your life in order to achieve the success that you wish you have. Because this is a fluid process, you may need to revisit different aspects over time as necessary in order to maintain your progress as well as set new goals.

For this journey, the most important tool you'll have is a 3-ring binder that you can use to record your thoughts, plans, visions and dreams. You can add sections to the binder that correspond to the different sections of this book or you can divide the binder into different aspects of your life that you want to address or you can divide the binder into different sections that represent different times that you revisit this process. The way you organize the binder isn't as important as your commitment to the process that the binder represents.

Now revisit each of the six chapters presented in this book and take the time to review the concepts in light of your own life. There are two steps that you will take with each chapter: 1) identify what currently exists—take an honest assessment of your life as it is to record what is your current reality and 2) identify the new reality of success that you want to see in each area in order to use this new vision as your "goal line" to be achieved. Take the time to reflect on each chapter, ask yourself the questions that are posed, complete the exercise and activities presented, and use your "goal lines" to develop your new actions and habits that will ultimately lead to your new life.

> **Note 2 Self: Opportunities are always around us. They only become options if we're prepared to actually act on them. ~KARS**

Every day is an opportunity to either be and get what you want out of life, or to remain the same. You have an opportunity presented to you in this book to change your life and become a creator of your success. Whether it takes 12 days, 12 weeks or 12 months—the decision and the process is yours as to how you address each area and the amount of time that you devote to them.

Just because things are presented in the book in a certain order doesn't mean that you have to address them that way.

Initially it may be easier to follow the sequence of things as outlined, but if your biggest stumbling point is fear, then you need to focus your initial efforts on the chapter dealing with Evicting the Element of Fear. If you're surrounded by toxic people then you want to begin with the chapter on Building the Team that you need. The beauty of this process is that it's YOUR PROCESS. YOU make the decisions about what areas of your life to focus on; YOU determine your Mind Movie of Success and subsequently outline your action plan to achieve it and YOU are the one who takes control of your life and becomes a CREATOR of your own success.

Life is a journey.

The things that happen during that journey are just way-points along the road that you travel. Nothing that has happened to you or will happen to you defines you. Who you are and what you become are ultimately left up to you to create.

~It's never too late to be who you want to become.~

Your life as a Creator of your success begins now. Make it count.

ABOUT THE AUTHOR

Keisha A. Rivers-Shorty is the founder and managing consultant of The KARS Group, LTD, specializing in providing personal and professional strategic development services to small businesses, organizations and individuals. She is also the founder and Executive  Director of The KARS Institute for Learning & Collaboration, a nonprofit organization whose mission is to provide training, resources and support to nonprofits, community organizations, churches, schools, and small businesses. She is a grant writer, adjunct instructor, former foundation executive director, educator and administrator.

She is a motivational and inspirational speaker, published author, and holds a Bachelor's degree in Elementary Education from the University of Pennsylvania, Master's degree in Curriculum & Instruction with a concentration in Teacher Leadership & Instruction from the University of New Orleans and is pursuing a PhD in Learning, Instruction & Innovation from Walden University.

A gifted motivational speaker, facilitator and trainer, attendees at her events have remarked at her passion, professionalism, talent, creativity and ability to communicate that not only educates, but inspires action. It is this undeniable belief in what's possible and the passion with which she communicates that belief that enables her to assist her clients in finding ways to make the possible more probable and the probable therefore doable. Using this approach, she has created a personal and professional strategic development model for women aptly entitled "Release Yourself" that is being implemented through the "Release Yourself Series[TM]" and "Released & Ready Tour[TM]" that is assisting clients across the country fuel their passion; align with their purpose and build their legacy through reflecting on their patterns; refining their thinking; rejuvenating their spirit; redirecting their path and releasing themselves to act. Visit www.karsgroup.com, www.releasedandready.com and www.karsinstitute.org for additional information about the company, programs and services.

BE THE CREATOR OF YOUR SUCCESS

Released & Ready™

Released & Ready is not just another "self-help" or motivational program.

It's not another "coaching group" or inspirational journey that you're about to embark upon with claims to "change your life'.

What it is--is a strategic, systematic approach to:

1. walking you through the process of identifying patterns in your life;
2. developing strategies for dealing with them and
3. implementing a sound action plan for getting to the success that you want to achieve

> *Note 2 Self: You need to have the sun set on your fears and self-imposed limitations in order to experience the dawning of new possibilities. ~ KARS | www.releasedandready.com*

Join the Released & Ready™ Series Programs visit www.releasedandready.com

Welcome to The KARS Group, LTD
Knowledge Always Reigns Supreme!

Information is static, knowledge is dynamic. You can have all of the information you want at your fingertips, but until you actively *apply* that information, you don't have true knowledge. At The KARS Group, LTD, we specialize in the process of facilitating knowledge acquisition for our clients. It's not enough to provide consulting but we focus on combining that with training and strategic development in order to provide opportunities for both personal and professional growth.

Because we understand what people go through who have experienced a deep longing and sense of wanting more in their lives, we've created an approach that provides support, development, education and encouragement. Our services are about more than simply completing paperwork for a small business or creating an organizational plan for a new nonprofit. It goes beyond providing step by step directions on how to navigate social media or complete a grant application.

What we provide at The KARS Group, LTD is a pathway to dynamic knowledge.

We don't provide you with all of the answers, but instead, we teach you the process of understanding what questions to ask so that you can seek out answers and discover solutions long after we're gone.

Our greatest triumph and accomplishment is to create a community of learners, collaborators and knowledge-seekers. It is our goal to assist our clients by providing them with services, support, training and development to enable them to *fuel their passion, align with their purpose and build their legacy*.

We do this by addressing three areas:
1. **Knowledge of Self**–Assisting clients to fuel their passion through our Released & Ready series of personal growth and development.
2. **Knowledge of Strategies**–Providing tools to assist clients to align with their purpose by enhancing their knowledge of strategy through our BeastMode Boot Camps.
3. **Knowledge of Systems**–Providing training and instruction that enables clients to building their legacy through understanding the systems required for success through The KARS Institute.

www.karsgroup.com

www.ingramcontent.com/pod-product-compliance
Lightning Source LLC
Chambersburg PA
CBHW021024090426
42738CB00007B/889